THE STORY OF JACKIE ROBINSON

A Biography Book for New Readers

Written by
ANDREA THORPE

Illustrated by
ANGIE ALAPE

ROCKRIDGE PRESS

For Donovan and all the other little children with big baseball dreams!

For general information on our other products and services or to obtain technical support, please contact our Customer Care Department within the United States at (866) 744-2665, or outside the United States at (510) 253-0500.

Rockridge Press publishes its books in a variety of electronic and print formats. Some content that appears in print may not be available in electronic books, and vice versa.

Series Designer: Angela Navarra
Interior and Cover Designer: Elizabeth Zuhl
Art Producer: Hannah Dickerson

Editor: Mary Colgan
Production Editor: Mia Moran
Production Manager: Holly Haydash

Illustrations © 2021 Angie Alape. Photography © Alpha Historica/Alamy Stock Photo, p. 48; Science History Images/Alamy Stock Photo, pp. 49, 51. All maps used under license from Creative Market. Author photo courtesy of JT Thorpe.

ISBN: Print 978-1-64876-650-3 | eBook 978-1-64876-150-8

R02

Printed in China

CONTENTS

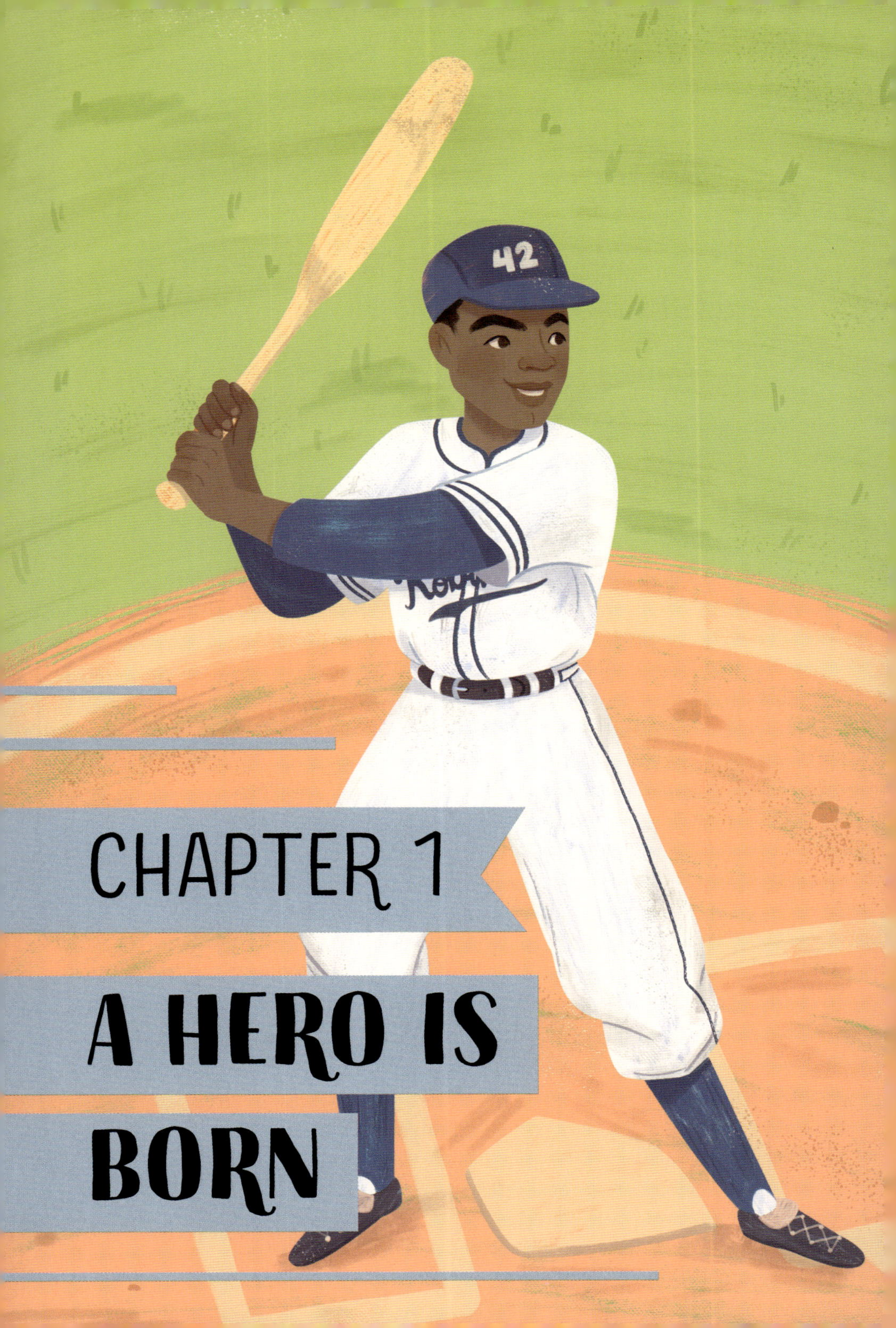

CHAPTER 1

A HERO IS BORN

Meet Jackie Robinson

Jackie Robinson loved to play ball. He grew up to be a baseball hero, but as a little boy he played any sport he could. Baseball, basketball, football, dodgeball . . . whatever the game, Jackie wanted to play and other kids wanted to play with him. At school, children would share their lunches with him if he agreed to join their team.

As Jackie grew older, he continued to play football, basketball, and especially baseball. Jackie played well, but being a Black baseball player was difficult. Black players were not treated kindly or fairly. Some white people wanted to keep sports **segregated**, so Black and white players could not play together. This made Jackie sad and angry. He knew things needed to change. He began to speak up about how unfairly Black people were treated.

As much as Jackie loved baseball, he also loved his family, especially his hardworking mother.

He didn't want her to have to work all the time, so Jackie found ways to earn money for his family. Whenever he had free time, Jackie did small jobs in the neighborhood. He even sold hot dogs at baseball games!

While growing up, Jackie Robinson faced many **challenges**. As a young boy, he had no idea that his excellent athletic skills and his helpful ways would make him famous one day. Jackie Robinson would become the first Black **Major League Baseball** player and a great **civil rights** leader!

Jackie's America

JUMP IN THE THINK TANK

Would you rather watch a sport or play a sport? Why?

Jack Roosevelt Robinson was born on January 31, 1919, in Cairo, Georgia. He was the youngest of five children. Many Black families, like the Robinsons, experienced **racism** living in Georgia. Racism is when someone mistreats another person because of their skin color.

Racism led to the creation of unfair **Jim Crow laws** that kept Black and white people separate. These cruel laws restricted the places Black

people could live, work, and play. Black people and white people could not eat in a restaurant together or swim in the same pool. When Black people rode on a bus, they were forced to sit in the back. Jim Crow laws also made it hard for Black families to find jobs and buy houses. The Robinsons decided to move across the country to Pasadena, California. Jackie's family hoped it would be easier to live there.

Life in Pasadena was better than life in Cairo. Jackie's mother was able to find work and purchase a house for her family, but racism and Jim Crow laws created problems in Pasadena, too.

MYTH	&	FACT
Black people only experienced racism if they lived in the South.		Racism in the Southern states was terrible, but Black people faced racism in all parts of the country.

WHEN?

Jackie is born.	The Robinsons move to Pasadena.
1919	**1920**

CHAPTER 2

THE EARLY YEARS

Growing Up

When Jackie was one year old, his father left. Jackie's mother, Mallie, had to raise five children on her own. The Robinson family lived in a house on Pepper Street in Pasadena. Jackie's mother made the house comfortable and planted a garden and some fruit trees. While Mallie worked during the day, Jackie's brothers and sister cared for him. Jackie loved all his siblings, but he was especially close to his sister, Willa Mae, and his brother Frank.

Most of the Robinsons' neighbors were white. Some of them were not happy to have a Black family living on Pepper Street. These neighbors were often unkind. The neighborhood children teased Jackie because he did not have a father. One time, a girl in the neighborhood called Jackie a terrible name because of his skin color. In town, Jackie's family was not allowed to swim in the town pool because they were Black.

Even though many people in Pasadena treated the Robinsons badly, Mallie would not allow her children to be unkind to them. She taught Jackie and her other children to be proud of who they were and to treat others with respect.

THE ROBINSON FAMILY

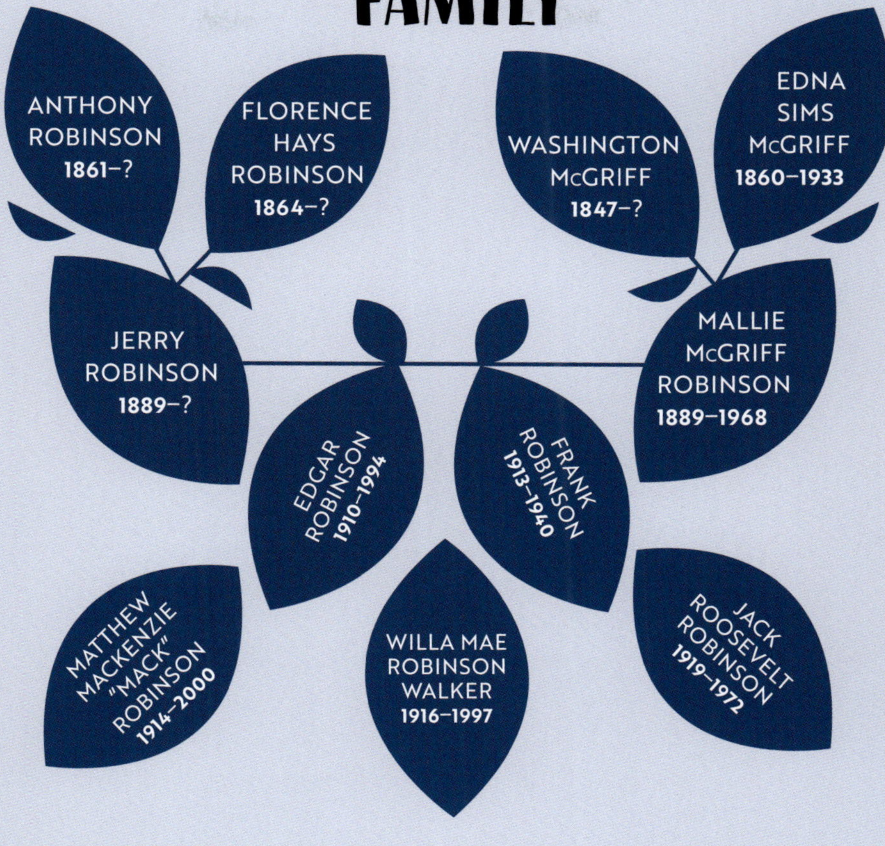

“I often thought about the **courage it took** for my mother to break away from the South.”

JUMP IN THE THINK TANK

Karl Downs helped Jackie when he was feeling bad and getting into trouble. Is there a family member or friend who encourages you when you feel upset?

A Young Athlete

Jackie was a terrific young **athlete**. He was a fast runner and often won when racing his friends and playing dodgeball. Jackie was great in any game he played—even marbles! When he got to high school, Jackie played baseball, football, and basketball. He did well in all three sports and was more and more **determined** to be a winning athlete.

A successful high school sports career didn't mean Jackie's life was always happy. When the **Great Depression** began in 1929, many people lost their jobs and were unable to buy the things they needed to live. Jackie's family struggled, but he made some money by cutting grass and delivering newspapers.

The Great Depression caused many people to feel sad and hopeless. Jackie and other teenagers in his neighborhood felt this way, too. They ended up forming the Pepper Street Gang. Soon, the gang was getting into trouble for stealing and playing pranks on people in the community.

Reverend Karl Downs was a good friend of the Robinson family. He talked to Jackie and reminded him that it was important to work hard in school and to stay out of trouble.

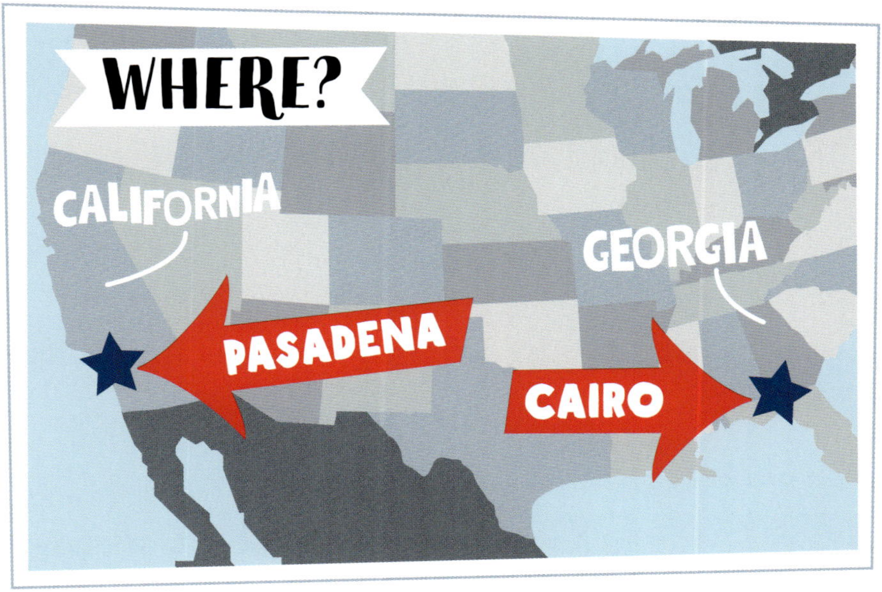

Reverend Downs played sports with Jackie and encouraged him to do well. Jackie listened and realized playing sports might help him succeed in life.

The Great Depression begins.

WHEN? **1929**

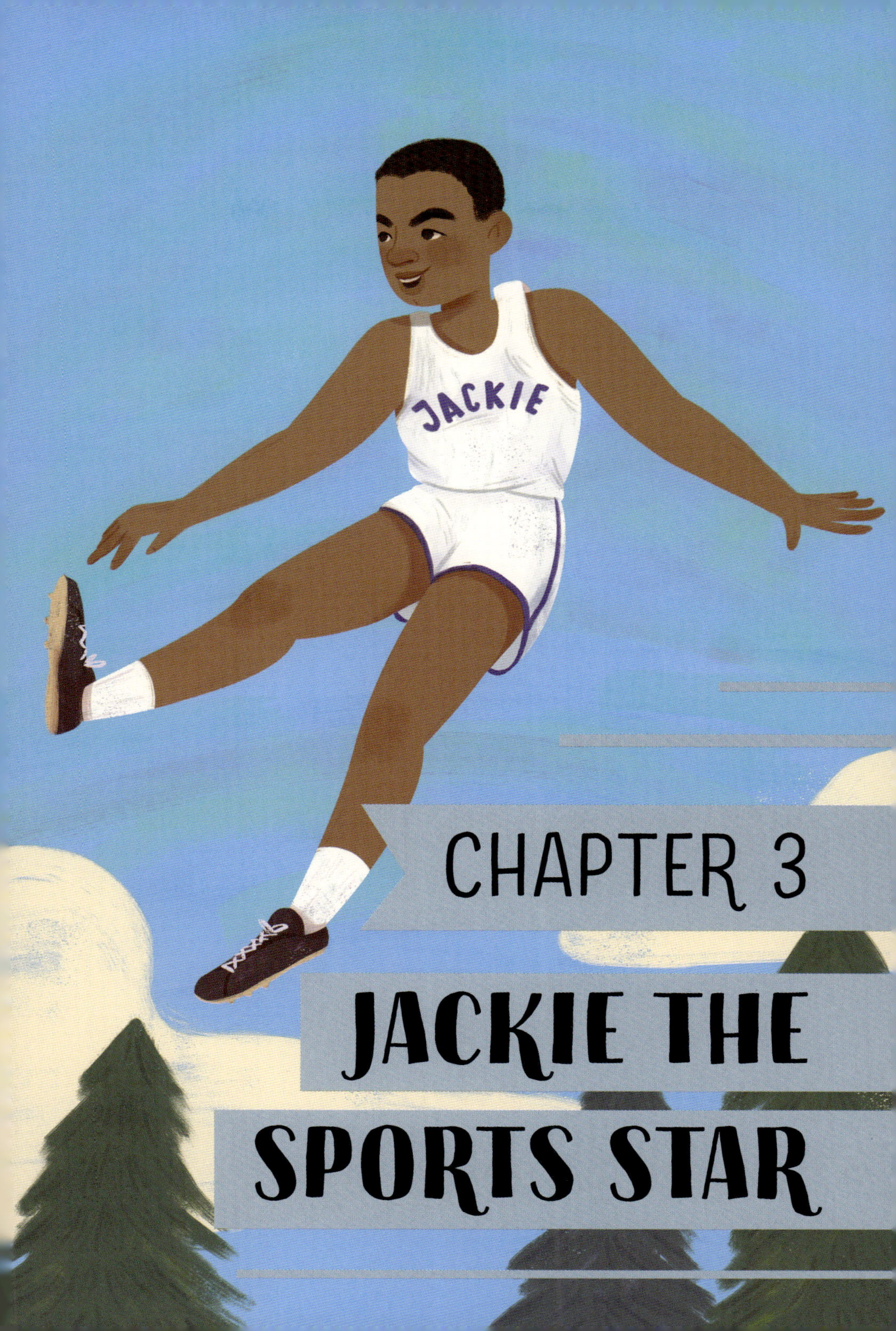

CHAPTER 3

JACKIE THE SPORTS STAR

A Way Out

In high school, Jackie played on the baseball, basketball, football, and track teams. Jackie's brothers wanted him to do well, so they encouraged him. Mack was an **elite** runner who had won a silver medal at the **Olympics**. He helped Jackie learn to run faster and catch better. Frank taught Jackie how to do well in school and how to stay focused on his goals.

Jackie continued to earn good grades and improve at sports. The local newspapers wrote about how well he played. Because of his hard work, Jackie earned a **scholarship** from the University of California, Los Angeles (UCLA). He was happy because he could stay close to home and go to a great college. But just after Jackie began college, something terrible happened. Jackie's brother Frank died in a motorcycle accident. Jackie was devastated.

He was determined to work harder so he could make his family proud. Jackie became the first UCLA athlete to get the school's highest awards in football, baseball, basketball, and track—and he did it all in just one sports season!

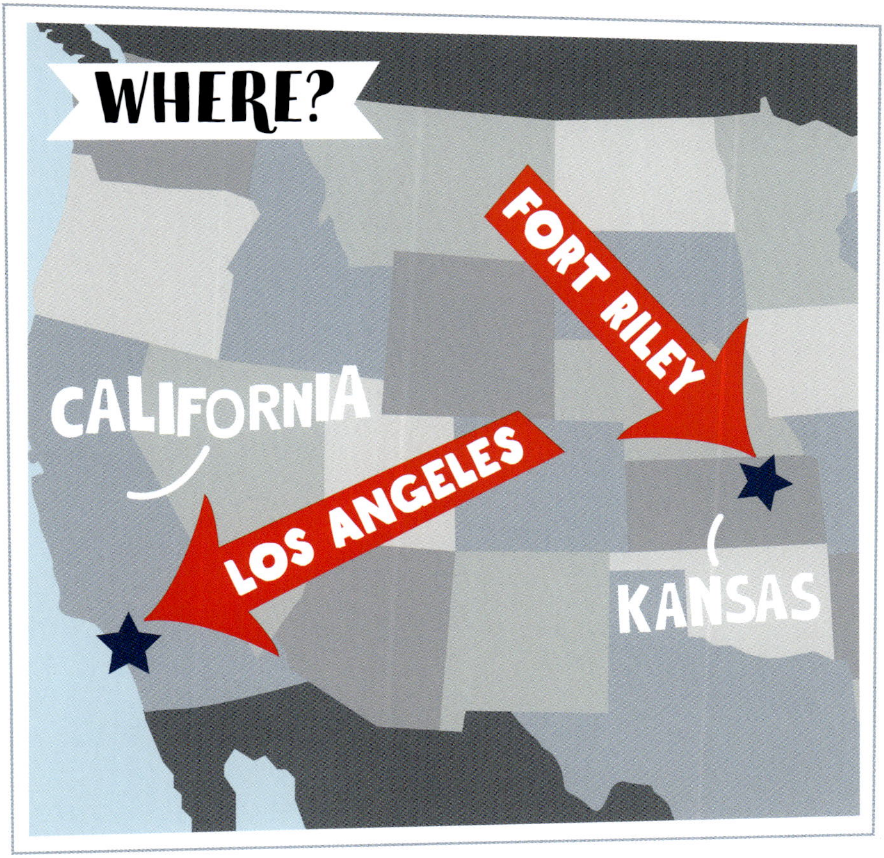

New Challenges

At UCLA, Jackie met many new people. Jackie's best friend introduced him to a young woman named Rachel Isum. Jackie thought she was smart, hardworking, and pretty. They became close friends and fell in love. She encouraged

Jackie to think about what he would like to do after college.

Jackie wanted to become a **professional** sports player, but segregation was still a big problem. None of the professional sports teams would hire a Black player. Jackie decided to leave UCLA to look for a good-paying job. This was difficult because Jim Crow laws still limited the jobs Black people could have.

In 1942, Jackie was drafted to the United States Army to serve in World War II.

JUMP IN THE THINK TANK

Jackie worked hard at school and at sports. How does hard work help people reach their dreams? How do you feel when you work hard at something?

MYTH & FACT

MYTH: Jackie Robinson **graduated** from UCLA in 1941.

FACT: Jackie Robinson did not graduate from UCLA because he left to find a job.

He was sent to training at Fort Riley in Kansas. Jackie thought Black people in the **military** would be treated fairly, but they were not. Black soldiers could not eat or work beside white soldiers. Jackie was angry when he learned Black soldiers could not play on the military's sports teams.

One evening, Jackie got onto a military bus. He did not sit in the back of the bus where Black people were supposed to sit. When the white bus driver told Jackie to move to the back of the bus, he refused. Jackie believed if he could serve his country during a war, he should be able to sit in any seat. Jackie was put on **trial** for refusing to move. He was found innocent, but Jackie was disappointed by what had happened. After the trial ended, Jackie left the military. It was time for him to look for another job.

WHEN?

1939 — Jackie starts college at UCLA.

1941 — Jackie leaves UCLA.

1942 — Jackie joins the Army.

CHAPTER 4
PLAYING BALL

The Negro Leagues

Near the end of Jackie's time with the Army, another soldier told Jackie his baseball team was looking for new players. This team, the Kansas City Monarchs, was part of the **Negro leagues**, which were professional baseball teams for Black players. (At the time, Black people were sometimes called Negroes, a term that is no longer used.)

Jackie joined the Kansas City Monarchs and quickly became the team's star **shortstop**. In the Negro leagues, Jackie met other great Black baseball players like Satchel Paige and Josh Gibson. Jackie loved baseball, but he did not like the late-night games. He did not like traveling to faraway places. He also missed Rachel.

Players in the Negro leagues used broken equipment, played on old fields, and got little pay. Black players had to eat meals outside and sleep on the team bus. This bothered Jackie.

He knew white professional baseball players were treated with respect. He wanted that for Black players, too.

Once, the team's bus stopped for gas at a white-owned gas station. Jackie wanted to use the restroom, but the owner said the restroom was only for white people. Jackie decided not to let the owner put gas in the bus. The owner knew he would lose money if the bus left, so he finally allowed Jackie to use the restroom.

These **injustices** made Jackie want to leave the Negro leagues. One day, he received a call from Branch Rickey, the president of the Brooklyn Dodgers, a Major League Baseball team.

MYTH &	FACT
There were not many Negro league teams.	There were more than 20 Negro league teams across the United States.

Branch wanted to talk to Jackie about a new opportunity in baseball. Jackie wanted to learn more, so he agreed to meet Branch in New York.

A New Opportunity

Branch Rickey was in charge of the Brooklyn Dodgers. He planned to **integrate** baseball and wanted Jackie to be the player to do it.

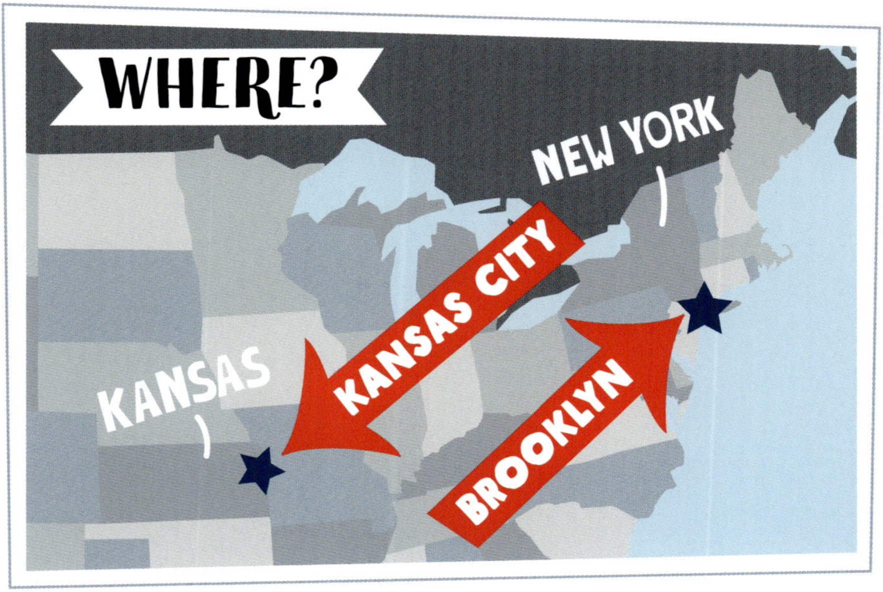

But Branch knew Major League Baseball's first Black player would face **criticism**. He warned Jackie about threats and name-calling. Branch wanted Jackie to understand that integrating baseball would be a huge challenge.

Branch asked Jackie if he would be able to stay calm in the face of cruel behavior. He believed if Jackie stayed focused on baseball and refused to fight back, other professional teams would accept Black players. Branch explained that Jackie would become a great **pioneer** and represent Black people all over the country.

Jackie had dreamed about playing for a major league team, so he carefully considered what this would mean. Jackie knew he would be upset by unfair treatment. He knew it would be hard not to fight back.

JUMP IN THE THINK TANK

If someone said mean things to you, would you be able to ignore them?

WHEN?

1945	1945	1946
Jackie plays for the Kansas City Monarchs.	Jackie joins the Montreal Royals.	Jackie and Rachel marry and have their son, Jackie Jr.

However, Jackie wanted to show that Black people were great athletes and great teammates. He agreed to sign Branch Rickey's **contract** and began playing for the Montreal Royals, the Dodgers' **minor league** team. The next year, Jackie and Rachel married and had their first child, a baby boy named Jackie Jr.

CHAPTER 5

THE MAJOR LEAGUES

Becoming a Dodger

While Jackie was playing with the Montreal Royals, his baseball skills improved even more. He also had to handle many insults. After Jackie played with the Royals for one season, Branch Rickey moved him up to the major leagues. On April 15, 1947, Jackie put on a Brooklyn Dodgers **uniform**. His number was 42. Jackie was nervous and excited as he stepped onto Ebbets Field and saw the huge crowd. He knew he had a big job to do, and he was ready to play. That day, Jackie Robinson broke the color **barrier** by becoming the first Black Major League Baseball player!

Jackie's early days as a Dodger were not easy. Jackie was now a first baseman. He had to work hard to play his new position well. Also, many of the other Dodgers did not want to play with a Black player. White players and fans continued to **harass** Jackie. He was called mean names. Some people even threatened to hurt Jackie and his family. During one game against the Philadelphia Phillies, the name-calling and insults were so terrible, Jackie lost his focus on the game. This upset Jackie. Sometimes he wanted to give up, but Jackie refused to quit!

JUMP IN THE THINK TANK

Have you ever wanted to give up when doing something hard?

He kept working hard because he loved baseball and he was determined to play well.

Jackie wanted to speak up for himself! But he kept his deal with Branch Rickey not to fight back against cruel treatment. He did not want to disappoint himself or Branch. Most of all, Jackie did not want to disappoint other Black players.

Rookie of the Year

Jackie worked hard and got better at hitting the ball and stealing bases. Large crowds came to watch him play. Jackie's teammates could not deny his talent and skills. They knew he helped make the Dodgers a winning team.

Over time, Jackie began to make friends with some of his teammates. One of his first friends was Pee Wee Reese. During a game in Boston, fans yelled at Pee Wee for being Jackie's friend. Pee Wee went to Jackie and placed his arm around Jackie's shoulders. This encouraged Jackie, and other Dodgers began to make friends with him, too.

> "I had started the season as a **lonely** man . . . I ended it feeling like a member of a **solid** team."

Jackie and his family moved to Brooklyn. Dodgers fans loved Jackie because he was an amazing athlete and a kind man. Jackie took time to greet his fans and sign autographs for them. He loved talking to children, who saw him as a role model.

In 1947, Jackie helped lead the Dodgers to the World Series, baseball's championship game.

Jackie was excited. His mother, Mallie, flew to New York to watch him play. The Dodgers didn't win the World Series that year, but it was still a fantastic year for Jackie. He led the major leagues in hits and stolen bases. He was the first player to win the new **Rookie** of the Year Award. Jackie was also featured on the cover of *Time* magazine. He had become a sports celebrity!

WHEN?

Jackie joins the Brooklyn Dodgers.
1947

Jackie becomes Rookie of the Year.
1947

Jackie is on the cover of *Time* magazine.
1947

CHAPTER 6

NUMBER 42

Most Valuable Player

Once Jackie broke the color barrier, more Black players were signed to major league teams. Jackie was happy because he could finally see the results of his hard work and **sacrifice**. After two successful baseball seasons, Branch Rickey told Jackie he could speak up and defend himself. Branch knew it was important for Jackie to speak out against injustice.

Now Jackie could respond differently to racism. If a player tried to hurt him on purpose, Jackie **confronted** him. If Jackie wasn't pleased with an umpire's unfair call, he said so. When newspaper reporters interviewed Jackie, he told them about the injustices he experienced. Jackie was no longer the quiet baseball player they once knew.

Jackie's talent and effort helped **unite** the Brooklyn Dodgers. The team players respected one another and worked well together. In 1949, the Dodgers made it to the World Series once again.

JUMP
–IN THE– THINK TANK

What did it mean for Jackie to be a role model for younger players? Do you want to be a role model for younger people someday?

The Dodgers did not win, but Jackie was named Most Valuable Player (MVP). He was recognized as the player who had worked the hardest to make the team successful.

Soon the Robinsons had a few more reasons to celebrate. Their family was growing! While living in Queens, New York, the Robinsons had two more children, Sharon and David. Jackie and Rachel wanted a better house for their family, so they moved to Stamford, Connecticut.

Standing Up for What's Right

Jackie played with the Dodgers for 10 years. Even though baseball was now integrated, there was still segregation in the South. When the Dodgers played in Southern states, Jackie was not allowed to enter restaurants and hotels. During games, Southern umpires often made unfair calls against Jackie. This made Jackie angry, and he always told the umpires how he felt about their behavior.

During the 1950s and 1960s, many Black people and some white people joined the **civil rights movement** to end racial **discrimination**. Jackie spoke about injustice and equal rights during **protests**. Jackie's words made some people uncomfortable. However, younger baseball players wanted to hear what Jackie had to say.

> "It felt good to be able to breathe freely, to speak out when I wanted to."

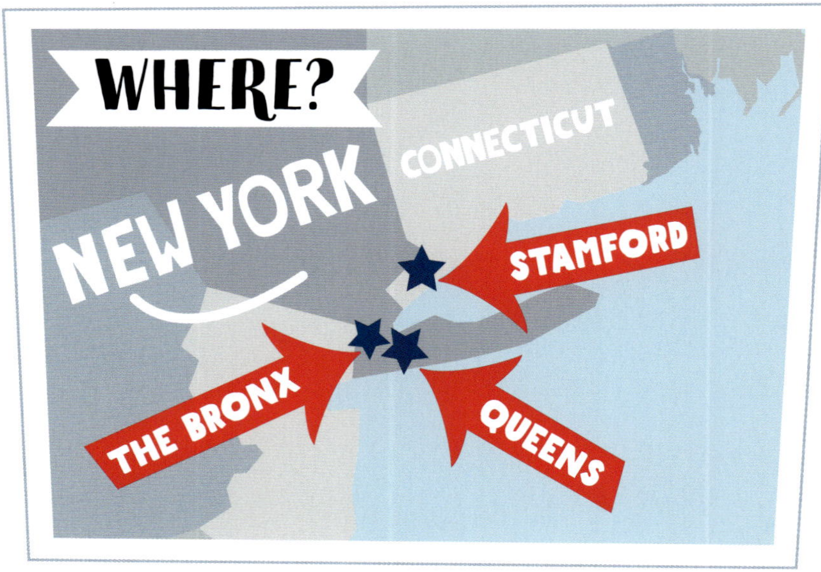

During his career, Jackie accomplished many great things. He led the **National League** in stolen bases. He was also chosen to be part of the National League All-Star Team several times. Jackie led the Dodgers to six championship games, and in 1955, he helped the team win the World Series at Yankee Stadium in Bronx, New York. In 1957, Jackie made a big decision. He **retired** from baseball. Jackie wanted to help Black people gain equal rights. He also wanted to spend more time with his family.

WHEN?

1949	1954	1955	1957
Jackie wins the Most Valuable Player Award.	The civil rights movement begins.	The Brooklyn Dodgers win the World Series.	Jackie retires from baseball.

CHAPTER 7

JACKIE THE LEGEND

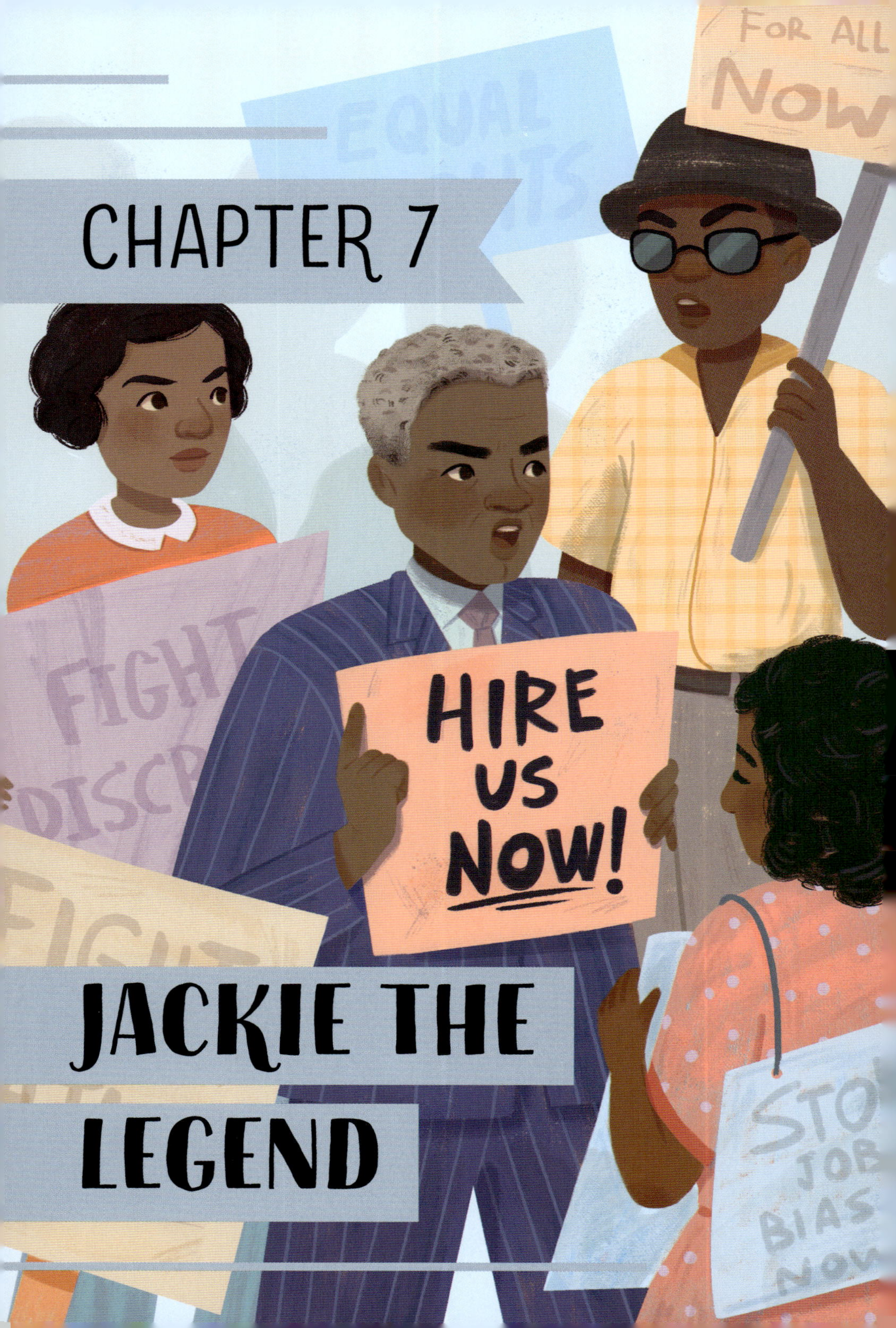

Breaking Barriers

During the civil rights movement, Jackie joined a group called the **National Association for the Advancement of Colored People (NAACP)**. NAACP members planned meetings and held **rallies** to help Black people gain equal rights. Jackie gave speeches about school integration. He wanted Black and white children to go to school together. Jackie also marched while carrying a sign that read "Hire Us Now!" Jackie even marched in the streets with famous civil rights leader Martin Luther King Jr. Jackie met with important political leaders and asked them to help the civil rights movement. As Jackie worked, Rachel was by his side.

Jackie still had a successful career, too. In 1965, he became the first Black man to work as an **announcer** for Major League Baseball. Jackie showed everyone that a Black man could do a great job explaining baseball games. Jackie also worked as a newspaper writer for the *New York Post*. He enjoyed writing articles that encouraged baseball teams to hire Black managers and coaches.

In 1962, Jackie received Major League Baseball's highest honor. He was the first Black player inducted into the Baseball Hall of Fame in Cooperstown, New York. His family and friends traveled to attend the ceremony. Jackie Robinson was now recognized as one of the best players in baseball history!

Jackie's Legacy

Jackie traveled around the country to work toward civil rights, but he was still a baseball hero. On October 15, 1972, when Jackie was 53 years old, Major League Baseball gave him another honor. He was invited to throw out the first pitch at the World Series. Jackie smiled and waved as he stepped onto the field. The large crowd stood, clapped, and cheered for Jackie as he threw the pitch. Jackie felt proud because baseball fans still remembered his hard work and accomplishments.

JUMP IN THE THINK TANK

If you were Jackie Robinson, how do you think it would feel to get into the Hall of Fame?

After a long baseball career and years of civil rights service, Jackie Robinson died shortly after on October 24, 1972.

Today, the world still remembers and honors Jackie Robinson. In 1984, Rachel accepted the Presidential Medal of Freedom for Jackie. In 1997, Major League Baseball honored Jackie by retiring his number. When a player's number is retired, it can never be assigned to another player. The number 42 would always be Jackie's special number. However, each year on April 15, now known as Jackie Robinson Day, every baseball player on every team wears the number 42 to celebrate Jackie. Rachel honors Jackie by continuing the civil rights work he began.

> "There is **not** an American in this country free until **every one** of us is free."

Jackie Robinson is an important part of American history. He will be remembered as a man who was not afraid to do hard things. He is honored for paving the way for countless others. Jackie Robinson changed the world!

WHEN?

1959 — Jackie becomes a writer for the *New York Post*.

1962 — Jackie is inducted into the Baseball Hall of Fame.

1965 — Jackie becomes a baseball announcer.

1972 — Jackie dies.

1997 — Jackie's number is retired.

CHAPTER 8

SO . . . WHO WAS JACKIE ROBINSON?

Challenge Accepted!

Now that you have learned all about Jackie Robinson's amazing life, let's test your new knowledge in a little who, what, when, where, why, and how quiz. Feel free to look back in the text to find the answers if you need to, but try to remember first!

1 Who was the civil rights leader that Jackie marched with?

- A Martin Luther King Jr.
- B Barack Obama
- C Branch Rickey
- D Frederick Douglass

2 Who was Jackie's wife?

- A Rebecca
- B Sarah
- C Maddie
- D Rachel

3 How did Jackie help the civil rights movement?

- A He participated in civil rights marches.
- B He wrote books about civil rights.
- C He taught college classes about civil rights.
- D He opened a civil rights museum.

4 What was Jackie's uniform number?

- A 29
- B 42
- C 11
- D 57

5 What Major League Baseball team did Jackie play for?

- A The Philadelphia Phillies
- B The Boston Red Sox
- C The New York Yankees
- D The Brooklyn Dodgers

6 **Where was Jackie born?**

- A Cairo, Georgia
- B Harlem, New York
- C Houston, Texas
- D Pasadena, California

7 **Why was April 15, 1947, such an important day?**

- A Jackie broke baseball's color barrier.
- B Jackie became the highest-paid baseball player ever.
- C Jackie retired from baseball.
- D Jackie got married.

8 **How did Jackie help the younger baseball players who came after him?**

- A He gave them money.
- B He let them stay at his house.
- C He encouraged them to work hard.
- D He wrote letters to them.

9 How is Jackie honored on Jackie Robinson Day?

→ A Players sing a song about Jackie.

→ B Players march in a parade.

→ C Players wear his number.

→ D Players write letters to Jackie's family.

10 When did Jackie retire?

→ A 1942

→ B 1984

→ C 1969

→ D 1957

Answers: 1. A; 2. D; 3. A; 4. B; 5. D; 6. A; 7. A; 8. C; 9. C; 10. D

Our World

Jackie Robinson's work changed our world! What are some things we have learned because of him?

- → Jackie showed that Black athletes are intelligent and skillful players who can compete in major league sports.
- → Jackie convinced others that civil rights such as equal pay and integrated schools are good for everyone.
- → Jackie proved that people can have successful careers in many areas, such as sports, business, and writing.

JUMP IN THE THINK TANK FOR MORE!

Put on your thinking hat! Let's think about some of the things Jackie Robinson did and consider how his legacy lives on.

- → Jackie Robinson broke the color barrier by becoming Major League Baseball's first Black player. What do you think would have happened if Jackie had not agreed to play for the Brooklyn Dodgers?

- → Jackie met with senators and presidents to discuss civil rights. Why do you think Jackie thought it was so important to speak to people in government about civil rights?

- → Jackie was a successful athlete, a strong civil rights leader, and a smart businessman. He was also a loving husband and father. What lessons do you think Jackie's family learned by watching him work?

Glossary

announcer: A person who gives information about an event on radio or television

athlete: A person who plays a sport

barrier: Something that blocks a person's way

challenge: A problem that someone tries to overcome

civil rights: Basic rights that every person has under the laws of the government to be treated fairly and equally

civil rights movement: A time of struggle during the 1950s and 1960s when Black people in the United States fought to end racial discrimination and have equal rights

confront: To meet someone face-to-face

contract: A written agreement

criticism: The act of speaking or showing disapproval

determined: Focused on reaching a certain goal no matter what

discrimination: The unfair treatment of a person or group of people

elite: Among the very best at something

graduate: To get a diploma or degree after completing school

Great Depression: A time in United States history when banks closed and many people lost their jobs

harass: To bother again and again

injustice: An act or behavior that is not fair, right, or equal

integrate: To end segregation

Jim Crow laws: Laws that enforced racial segregation following the end of slavery

Major League Baseball: The highest league in baseball

military: The United States' armed forces, which include the Army, Navy, and Air Force

minor league: The league below the major league

National Association for the Advancement of Colored People (NAACP): A civil rights organization that works to help maintain equal rights for Black people

National League: One of the two professional baseball leagues that make up Major League Baseball. The other is the American League.

Negro leagues: A group of professional baseball teams for Black players from the 1880s until the 1960s

Olympics: Athletic games held every four years where the best athletes from many countries compete in many sports

pioneer: Someone who does something for the first time

professional: Participating in an activity for pay

protest: The act of showing that you disagree with something, especially in public

racism: Discrimination against someone of a different race based on the belief that one's own race is superior

rallies: Large meetings where people come together to support a cause

retire: To leave a job after many years of work

rookie: A new member of a sports team

sacrifice: To give up something in order to get something else

scholarship: Money given to a student to pay for school

segregate: To separate people, usually based on their race or skin color

shortstop: A baseball player who catches balls between second and third base

trial: A court meeting to decide whether someone is innocent or guilty of a crime

uniform: Special clothing worn by people on the same team

unite: To join together

Bibliography

Eig, Jonathan. *Opening Day: The Story of Jackie Robinson's First Season*. New York: Simon & Schuster, 2008.

Rampersad, Arnold. *Jackie Robinson*. New York: Alfred A. Knopf, 1997.

Robinson, Jackie. *I Never Had It Made*. New York: Putnam, 1972.

Tygiel, Jules. *Baseball's Great Experiment: Jackie Robinson and His Legacy*. New York: Oxford University Press, 1983.

Acknowledgments

Jackie Robinson's determination, class, and courage are truly awe-inspiring. I am grateful for the opportunity to share his story with young readers and their families. Jackie stood up when others wanted him to sit down. He spoke up when others wanted him to be silent. Jackie's life made a difference and his amazing legacy lives on. Thank you, Number 42!

I am grateful for my husband and our three precious daughters. As I worked on this project, their daily encouragement blessed me beyond measure. I appreciate every hug, every kiss, every prayer, and every sweet word they offered me. Thank you for your love!

About the Author

ANDREA THORPE is a wife and the mother of three daughters. She has been homeschooling her children for 11 years. Before becoming a homeschool mom, Andrea earned a bachelor of arts degree in English and a master's degree in student personnel services. During her nine years in public education, Andrea worked as a classroom teacher and guidance counselor, and was recognized as Teacher of the Year. In her spare time, Andrea enjoys hanging out with family and friends, searching for bargains in antiques and thrift stores, and working on home decor projects.

About the Illustrator

ANGIE ALAPE was born in Colombia. She grew up drawing on every cardboard box around her, making all kinds of nonexistent worlds to play in with her siblings. She has been working as a freelance illustrator since her first collaboration with a Chilean editorial; recently, she has worked in editorial publishing, social campaigns, character design for 3D animation, and web magazines. In her spare time, you can find her playing with her adopted dogs and looking for places to enjoy a nice meal over the weekend.

WHO WILL INSPIRE YOU NEXT?

EXPLORE A WORLD OF HEROES AND ROLE MODELS IN ***THE STORY OF***... BIOGRAPHY SERIES FOR NEW READERS.

LOOK FOR THIS SERIES
WHEREVER BOOKS AND EBOOKS ARE SOLD

Alexander Hamilton
Albert Einstein
Martin Luther King Jr.
George Washington

Jane Goodall
Barack Obama
Helen Keller
Marie Curie